The Habit of Noticing

To Peter [signature]

Darden Smith
The Habit of Noticing
Using Creativity to Make a Life (and a Living)

About the Author

In a career spanning over three decades, singer-songwriter Darden Smith has released 15 critically acclaimed albums, composed a symphony, scored works for contemporary dance theater and written music for film, theater and advertising. He served a two-year appointment as artist-in-residence at Oklahoma State University's School of Entrepreneurship, and has brought collaborative songwriting to Fortune-500 companies to help capture their story and revitalize their culture. Smith also co-founded SongwritingWith:Soldiers, a nationally recognized nonprofit organization that brings professional songwriters together with wounded veterans to write songs based on their experiences of combat and the return home. Smith continues to write, record and perform, and spends a great deal of time drawing sketches without straight lines.

The Habit of Noticing
Using Creativity to Make a Life (and a Living)
By Darden Smith

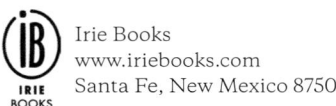 Irie Books
www.iriebooks.com
Santa Fe, New Mexico 87501

All text and images copyright © 2018 Darden Smith
Foreword copyright © 2018 Warren Zanes
All rights reserved
Printed in the United States of America
No part of this book may be used or reproduced in any manner without written permission except for brief quotations for review purposes only.
ISBN 978-15154-1717-0

Cover photo: Matt Lankes
Author photo: Michael O'Brien
Pages 2–3: Over Tennessee, 2014; Page 4: Footprints, San Francisco, 2013
Design by DJ Stout / Jeffrey Wolverton at Pentagram, Austin, Texas

dardensmith.com / songwritingwithsoldiers.org

For the late, great record man, Nigel Grainge,
Who never failed to be on fire.

CONTENTS

Foreword
Tiddlywinks *12*

Introduction
Twenty-Two-Dollar Guitar *16*

1. The Well
Inspiration

The Dream Curtain of Song *21*
Haydust *25*
A Bit of This, a Bit of That *26*
Tin Cans and Wire *29*
Your Mind Is a Sponge *30*
Keyhole *34*
Suggestion *37*
Adventure *38*
That Water *41*

2. The Circus
Influences

The Circus *44*
Leaving Town *49*
The Masters *50*
Mentors *52*
Get a Coach *53*
Artists and Benefactors *56*
Show Business *59*
Concrete *62*

3. No Plan B
Commitment

Johnny's Song *67*
A Hotel With a View of the Freeway *68*
Get in the Van *72*
The Disappearing Pop Star *73*
Music Is a Blue-Collar Gig *75*
Sleeping on Couches *76*
Get in or Get Out *80*
No Plan B *82*
Completely Unemployable *85*
Welding *86*
Process *91*
Play Music First *92*
Practice *95*
Scales and Demos *96*
Hunger *98*
Suffering for the Sake of Suffering *103*

4. The Habit of Noticing
Presence

Wake Up *106*
This Is Not a Mistake *109*
The Habit of Noticing *110*
Words Matter *114*
Collaboration *115*
Warren Barigian *116*
The House Manager *118*
Everything *121*

5. Do What You Do, Kid
Authenticity

Do What You Do, Kid *124*
Swimming *125*
Lists *129*
The Truth of Jean Cocteau *131*
Background Noise *132*
An Artist's Guide to Fashion *135*
Bells and Whistles *136*
Spin *137*
First You Have to Take Good Pictures *140*
D.L. Cerney *143*
Perfection Is Boring *145*
The Edge *148*

6. I'll See Your Talent and Raise You a Phone Call
Endurance

The Teasers *155*
Reviews *156*
It's Not the Magna Carta *159*
Stage Fright *160*
It'll Get Better *162*
Even if No One Hears It *166*
Fear of Not Being Brilliant *167*
The Water Tap *169*
Boredom *170*
Boxes *173*
I'll See Your Talent and Raise You a Phone Call *177*
Never Buy a Bus *178*
Luggage *181*
You Can't Eat an Art Burger *184*
Value *185*
Grand Canyon *186*
Finding the New Hat *189*
The Seven-Year Wave *192*

7. Echo
Meaning

Echo *198*
The Deal *201*
Art at All Costs *202*
Robert Henri *204*
Lifestyle *207*
My Real Work *209*
An Afternoon with Paul Williams *211*
The Party *214*
The Risk of the Plugged-In Life *217*
Fearing Your Gift *218*

Acknowledgments *224*

Following spread:
Marlboro Man, 2013,
Vista Caballo, 2014

INTRODUCTION
Twenty-Two-Dollar Guitar

A '67 Ford Country Squire station wagon moves north up a highway late on a central Texas Sunday evening. It is probably the spring, or early summer, of 1969. My parents' voices are a distant mumble from the front seat. My older brother and sister are asleep behind them. I sit by myself in the far back seat watching the headlights of the other cars move around us. The brittle sound of "Raindrops Keep Fallin' On My Head" comes out of the AM radio speaker. I strum along on the guitar I just bought from my brother for $22. And though I don't know how to play a single chord, I don't care. It sounds fantastic, right in time with the radio. I'm 7 years old and killing it.

The feeling I had that night — being on my own, separate, alone in the back of that big beast of a car, lost in the sound of the radio, the guitar notes against my parents faraway voices, the highway lights coming through the windows, moving against the dark of the backseat — is something I've been chasing all my life. It's the perception that I'm connected to a world bigger than my own, and though I don't understand it, it makes perfect sense. I recognized it then and pursued it even though I didn't know what I was doing. I turned that connection into a career, watching the details move, change, but all the while, the essence remained the same.

Music, sound, image, words ... and the stories they can tell.

I'm lucky (or unlucky, depending on your perspective) to pay my bills with songs. I worked hard, got some breaks, and kept going. At an early age, I learned that writing songs allows me to express thoughts I can't in other ways, to interpret what I see around me, to move people. And through it, I've become addicted to the very act of noticing. Then, using my creativity in all the forms I can possibly wrap my arms around, my job is to make some sense out of what I see. I think this is the main guiding motivator in my life. It's what keeps me on the planet.

From 2011 to 2013, I was an artist-in-residence at Oklahoma State University. Over the course of my time there, I began to see a pattern in the stories I would tell the students. I found myself noting repeatedly that the creative life is full of struggle; it's not for the faint of heart, but the payoff can be beautiful; that art and music are business — and that, like any business, we start out with a dream, stumble against blocks in the path, have success, watch it slip away, and (hopefully) earn it back again. Like everyone else, we sometimes lose sight of the original vision, only to find it again, and again; we evolve or fade away. We deal with the same issues as every enterprise, but just have a different way of coping with the problems and figuring out answers.

I didn't set out to write a how-to manual on creativity, or a book on process. This isn't a straight narrative, or even linear, for that matter. These stories trace my own personal arc from being that kid in the back of the station wagon to the present. It's a collection of stories about where I come from, what I've seen and heard as I've tried to figure out how to get along in the world, my inspirations and influences, the importance of commitment and endurance in tough times, why you should always be yourself, and the beauty that comes from finding meaning in your work and your life.

Though I'm not the most successful or famous artist on the planet, I'm pretty sure I am one. From my experience, working artists are people with heart and passion; hard workers, self-starters, doers. They wake up in the morning looking for a way to make a difference, to tell a story. They follow their words and dreams with action. They create. I was given a gift, yes, but was also helped along the way by mentors and teachers. Luck, good and bad, was always there when I needed it most. I have survived with my inspiration intact, and every day, fall more in love with writing songs. And though I've been playing music for three decades, put out a bunch of records and been to a lot of great cities, inside I'm still that 7-year-old boy sitting in the far back seat of a '67 Country Squire station wagon, strumming a $22 guitar, lost in the mystery, and hoping it never ends.

The story isn't over yet, but here's what I have so far.

1.
The Well
Inspiration

The Dream Curtain of Song

It's a weekday morning; let's call it Wednesday.
I'm 16, maybe 17 years old
Getting dressed for school and
Listening to the radio — KLOL-FM 101.
It's Houston, Texas in the late '70s.

Dylan's "Simple Twist Of Fate" comes on.
I stop, mesmerized.
Just the bass line is enough
To pull me in.

I sit there, dazed, on the edge of my bed, one shoe on, one shoe off,
Staring at the stereo, trying to figure this song out.
I can't. What's he singing about?
It comes at me through smoke
From another world, some hidden place.
And wherever it's coming from, I want to go there.

I've been writing songs since I was 10.
Guy Clark, Willie Nelson,
John Prine, Jerry Jeff Walker —
These are my guides.
Folk songs. Country. I've just discovered Townes Van Zandt.
And here comes Dylan
Knocking the legs out from under all I know
Telling the story backwards if at all,
Starting at the end, jumping to the beginning,
Details filled in as an afterthought.
I listen hard, thinking, how did he do that?
I want what he has.

That moment is an invitation into the mystery.
The song itself calls out, "Follow me."
And from that day on I do,
Down into the swirl of melody and words
Behind the dream curtain of song.

Storm, Maui, 2017

Following spread:
Lights on a Truck, NYC, 2016

The song itself calls

And from that day on

Down into the swirl

Behind the dream

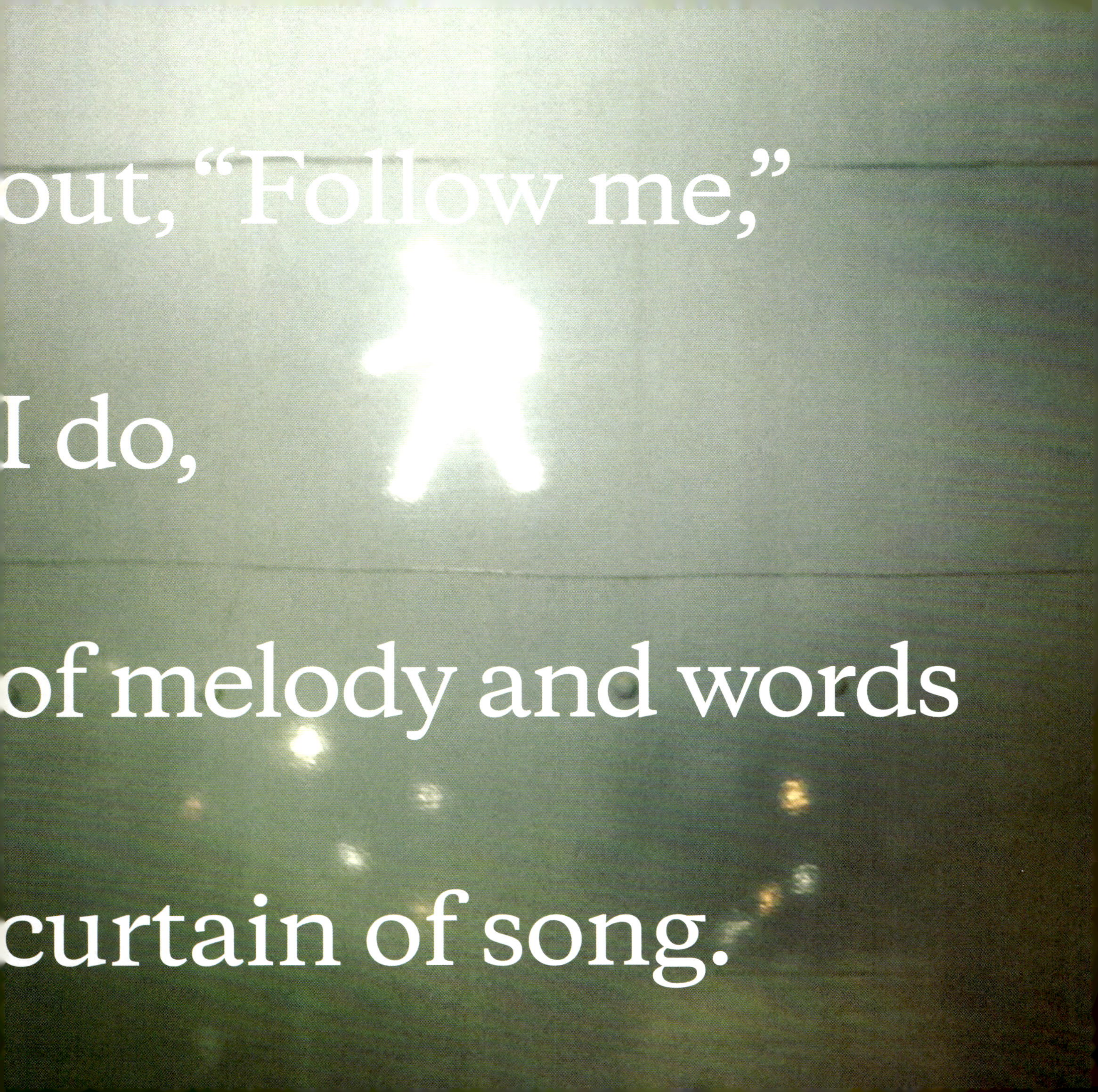

out, "Follow me,"

I do,

of melody and words

curtain of song.

Haydust

I am about 10 years old, standing in the second-floor hayloft of our barn, watching the sunlight come through the cracks in the wall. I pull the wire off the bales, break them into sections and push them down through the trap doors to the cattle below. Haydust gets caught in the updraft, rising, sparking like tiny floating stars.

Later, standing in the big door on the loft, looking out over the pens toward the pastures and woods beyond, the air is still, and I see dust from the hay harvest hanging in the lower part of the pasture, suspended, glowing in the late afternoon light.

I stay there till dusk fades to purple, then gray. I finish my chores, close the barn and walk slowly back to the house, singing a slow song. It's cold now. Night is coming. Crows fly home across the sky. I am blue before I even know what it means.

This is the day I first experience art.

Tree, Dulwich, 2016

A Bit of This, a Bit of That

Making art is like mixing a cocktail.
You take a bit of this, a bit of that, a memory, a feeling,
Maybe something someone said one time.
A photo, a dream.
Put everything in a glass. Stir it up.
What comes out is new.
Made from those disparate parts
But unique.

The hard part is knowing what to put in and what to leave out,
What to use today or hold back for tomorrow.
It takes time to learn the difference.

Firefly, 2014

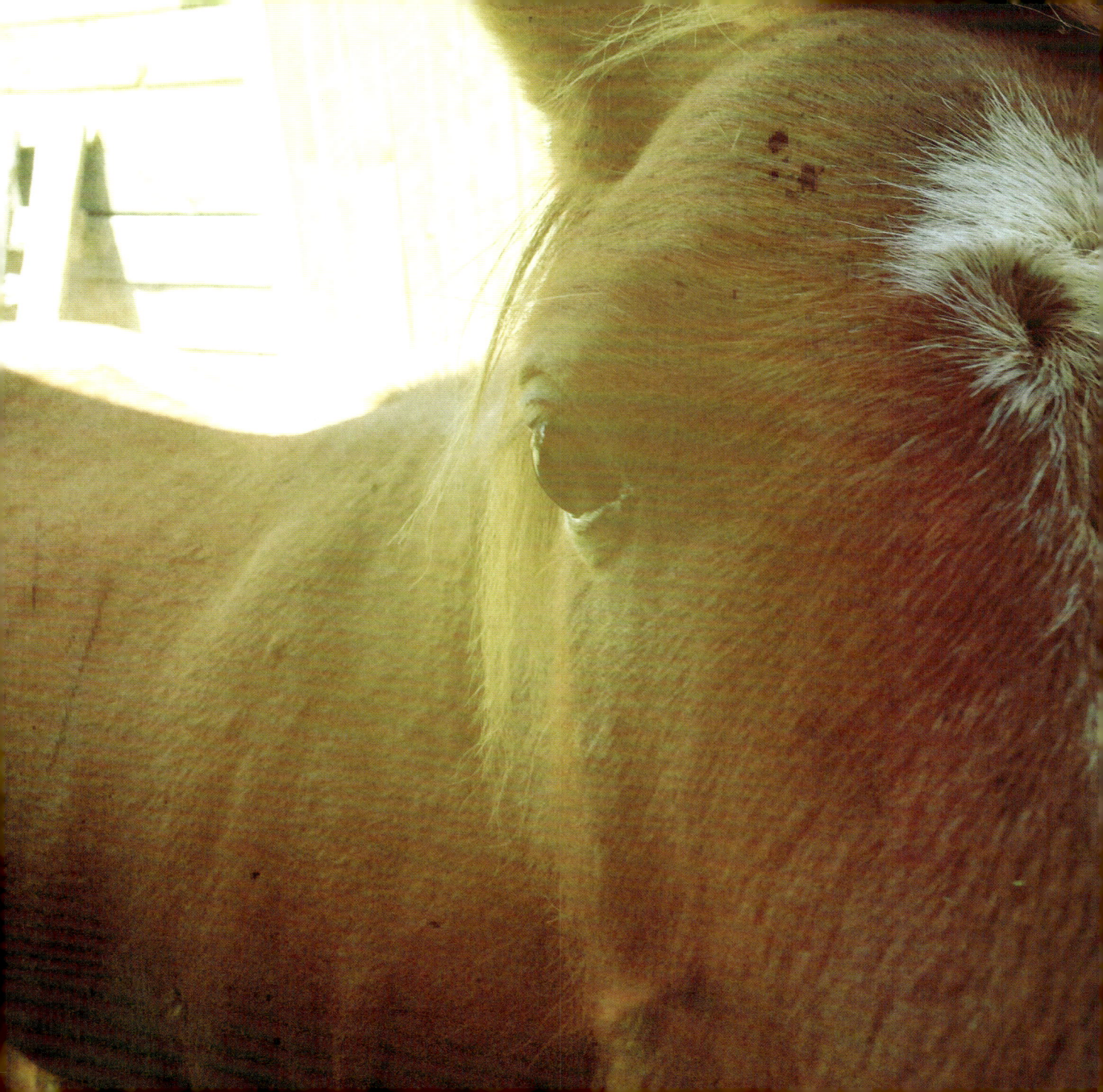

Tin Cans and Wire

Sephare, Botswana, 2012

Sitting on the porch
Of the house where we are staying
While doing a documentary,
I work on songs as two boys sit by the road
Playing with a toy made from
Tin cans and wire.

Lost in their games,
They laugh and talk
As rocks become houses and
Sticks change to people and cars.
Their minds fill the gap.

Their children's game is the purest form of art.
Raw imagination making a world from nothing.

Joseph, Sephare, 2012

Your Mind Is a Sponge

Your mind is a sponge
Built to absorb what's around you.

Creativity depends on keeping a box
Of ideas and sounds, images and emotions
Stored away in your brain
That you can call up at will
To reshape in your own vision,
To mold some sense from the
Rubble and noise.

Open your mind wide enough
To let the world come in.

Make it a practice, a habit.

Because without it, your artistic and human desires are
Leaning against a wall that's not there.
You're trying to squeeze water from
A dry sponge.

Lucky Strike, Paris, 2012

Following spread:
Bluemont, 2014

Keyhole

The next time you're in an old house, one with antique doors,
Put your eye up to the keyhole.
Notice the way your vision spreads out on the other side.
Back away, and the picture goes to nothing much at all.

This is the way of good songs, good paintings, a lover.
The closer you get, the more you can see.

I'm thinking of Springsteen's "I'm On Fire."
It's a tiny song. Fourteen lines.
But it paints a huge picture.

It fascinates me that someone can sit in a room miles and years from where I am
Put some words on a page, sing them, and when I hear the song
A movie starts running in my brain.

But it's not what the writer saw.
It's my vision alone, pulled from my life, my dreams, my past
Built on someone else's spark.

They put their eye to the keyhole
So I could see the world
On the other side of that door.

Falfurrias, Texas, 2016

Suggestion

The real accomplishment
Is to write a love song
And never say the word.

The suggestion of a line
Is often more powerful
Than the line itself.

Give just enough detail.
The audience is smarter than you think.

Kiss, 2015

Adventure

Summer, 1994

I'm the opening act on Stevie Nicks' summer tour.
For the three months that we cross the country
I know that a two-year odyssey of
Recording, travel, promotion and shows
Is coming to a close,
And I'm worried.
I don't have songs for a new record.
Not sure if I have anything to say.

Backstage at some amphitheater out west,
Maybe in San Francisco, or San Jose,
The drummer in Stevie's band, Russ Kunkel,
Tells me I should go on an adventure,
Drive across the country,
Do anything to shake the trees.

What he's saying is I need to
Get out of my mind.
See something new,
Go find the songs.

Shortly after that tour, I go completely off the rails
With a divorce-money-career collapse
And I start to question who I am
As a man, a father, an artist.
But instead of running from the chaos, I dive down into it.
Writing, always writing.
And from those upside-down days
I find a whole new bag of songs,
A new vein to explore.

Over the next few years
I come to see that
The real adventure is inside the walls of my own house,
My own soul.
I stop hiding in my songs,
And start telling the truth.

Russ is right.
Sometimes we need to take an adventure,
Blow the carbon off the spark plugs,
Trick ourselves into seeing what's really there.

That Water

They say there's a river running underneath
This town, but I don't know where
They say there's a river running underneath
This town, but I don't know where
Tell me how far, tell me how long
Where it got started, what went wrong
I got to find it
I got to find it
I want a drink of that water

Everyman's got something down inside
Some story he's afraid to tell
Everyman's got something down inside
Could be a ticket to hell
You got yours, I got mine
I ain't talked about in a long, long time
I got to find it
I got to find it
I want a drink of that water

So what makes a man fall in love with a mountain
A mountain too big to climb
I guess everybody got have something
He's not afraid to die trying to prove
I got to find it
I got to find it
I want a drink of that water

It might run deep, might run slow
Where does it come from, where does it go
Did the angel weep, did the devil cry
Did the earth just sigh
I got to find it
I got to find it
I want a drink of that water

Creek, 2016

From the 2013 album, Marathon

2.
The Circus
Influences

The Circus

I like a circus crowd.
Those a step outside the norm.
Music, food, theater, film people,
Writers, photographers, painters ... the list goes on.
Put them on a stage, at a desk with a pen, behind a stove, a camera
And they'll tell you a story that can break your soul, or
Make you lose yourself in love.

They're full of what makes the world entrancing.
Walking close to an edge that I recognize
And lean toward myself,
They're my guides, inspirations, teachers,
Making a living — a life — with a paintbrush or a guitar,
They traffic in the mystery.

Being around that circle helps me
Better know how to touch both
The burning joy and
The dark secrets
Of this world

And to be always arcing toward the better, the deeper.

Joe Ely is the only person I know
Who ran off and joined an actual circus.
Talk to him about that time even now
And his eyes light up.

Few of us can go that far.
But look around.
Find your own circus.

That place,
That gang
That draws
You slowly, slowly out
Onto your own
Highwire.

Joe Ely, 2018

Following spread:
Crop Circles, West Texas, 2010

"Art is about

leaving town."

— Terry Allen

Leaving Town

I'm in artist and songwriter Terry Allen's studio in Santa Fe.
The room is huge, full of light.
Tables holding different projects are scattered around —
Sculpture, drawings, song lyrics,
Props for an upcoming theater piece.

He tells me, "Art is about leaving town. I always wanted to be a leaver."

I think he means you need to know where you come from,
Whether it's a place, or just a mindset.
You have to be clear about that before you can truly go anywhere worthwhile.

The first place is comfortable.
The middle is exciting, scary; maybe a few wrong turns. The unexpected.
The end is unknown. Fresh.

You have to be willing to wander.
And when you finally arrive, don't get too comfortable.
It's not forever. One day you will have to leave again.

I'm not interested in artists who do the same thing all the time.
I want to see something new.

And one day I want to grow up to be Terry Allen.

Terry Allen, 2015

The Masters

Work with the masters.
Find them where they are.
Watch, listen, take them in

With their roaming desire to pass on what they've learned
Even though they sometimes aren't truly clear
And can't put into words all they know.
Believe me, they are looking for someone
Who is interested in what they have to share.

Absorb their history, their stories,
The essence of their life and work.
Keep it in your pocket
Like a stone from a far-off river
So that years down the line,
Hunched over a song lyric in a hotel room
You can bring it out, put it on the table

And that secret, carried all this time
Can be the key to your new chorus.

My own masters are not only songwriters, but producers, players, marketing people, photographers, filmmakers, chefs, soldiers, my own father. It has nothing to do with notoriety, and everything to do with spirit.

Man, Frome, 2017

Mentors

Certain bits of knowledge
Can only be passed to you subtly,
Like secrets between spies
Crossing a hotel lobby.
A whisper, a word
From one who has been through the lines
And now sits across from you
At exactly the right time
With the precise information you need.

In my early years, I don't have mentors.
But once I start to find them,
And to slow down enough to listen,
The maps I crave
Begin falling into my pocket.

And I carry their fragments still.
Pulling them out when I come to a crossroad,
They show me how to be, when to change,
Whom to pursue, what to leave behind.

A mentor changes your polarity
With the irrevocable seeping of insight
From their life to yours.

Take it in.
Tomorrow, it might be your turn to share the secret.

Get a Coach

If you're a basketball player
And suddenly lose control of your free throws
You're not going to just stand there and shoot the ball,
Hoping your aim miraculously gets better.

No, you would get a coach.

It's not always possible to recognize
What's holding you back,
Pushing you sideways or blocking your way.
You can't see the whole picture while
Standing in the middle of your own circle.

If you want to get better,
To move forward,
Eventually, you're going to need help.
Ask. It's there, waiting.

Following spread:
Paris Doors, 2018

Artists and Benefactors

Artists need benefactors
But it works the other way as well.
Benefactors need artists.
It's mutual.

Artists need funds to make their work happen.
And those with financial resources can't always make the film,
Paint the painting, create the dance.
But they still long to be involved, connected.

A benefactor once tells me, "Money is energy."
I would turn it around and say that art is energy.
Put the two together and light up the sky.
Successful artist/benefactor relationships are collaborations
With everyone contributing what they can.

There's no savior. No saved. No one is more or less than the other.
There's just an abundance of possibility and wonder
At what can be created by coming together.

Man in a London Cafe, 2015

Show Business

As a boy, my father occasionally takes me out of school and we go to the local cattle auction.
It is infinitely more interesting than anything happening in the fourth grade.

The show starts in the cafe before the auction
And continues on during the parade of cows, calves, heifers and bulls,
Ending only with the loading of trailers late in the afternoon.

Sitting beside him, I marvel at the noise, the smells, the cowboy hats and cigarettes,
The sing-song of the auctioneer.
I watch the men brag, go quiet, laugh, tell obvious lies about the livestock,
Always angling for the upper hand.

There's an old rancher that often sits next to us.
He puts his left arm around my shoulder,
Tells me dirty jokes and tries to convince me to buy the most ragged cattle.
Later, in the car, my father explains how the old man is using me
As a screen to hide his bids from the guy sitting on his right side.

It's a performance.
Whether it's one man in a room with canvas and paint, a songwriter on a stage
Or some old rancher talking shit in the cafe at the auction barn,

All business is show business.

Bull, 2016

Following spread:
Leaves, NYC, 2013

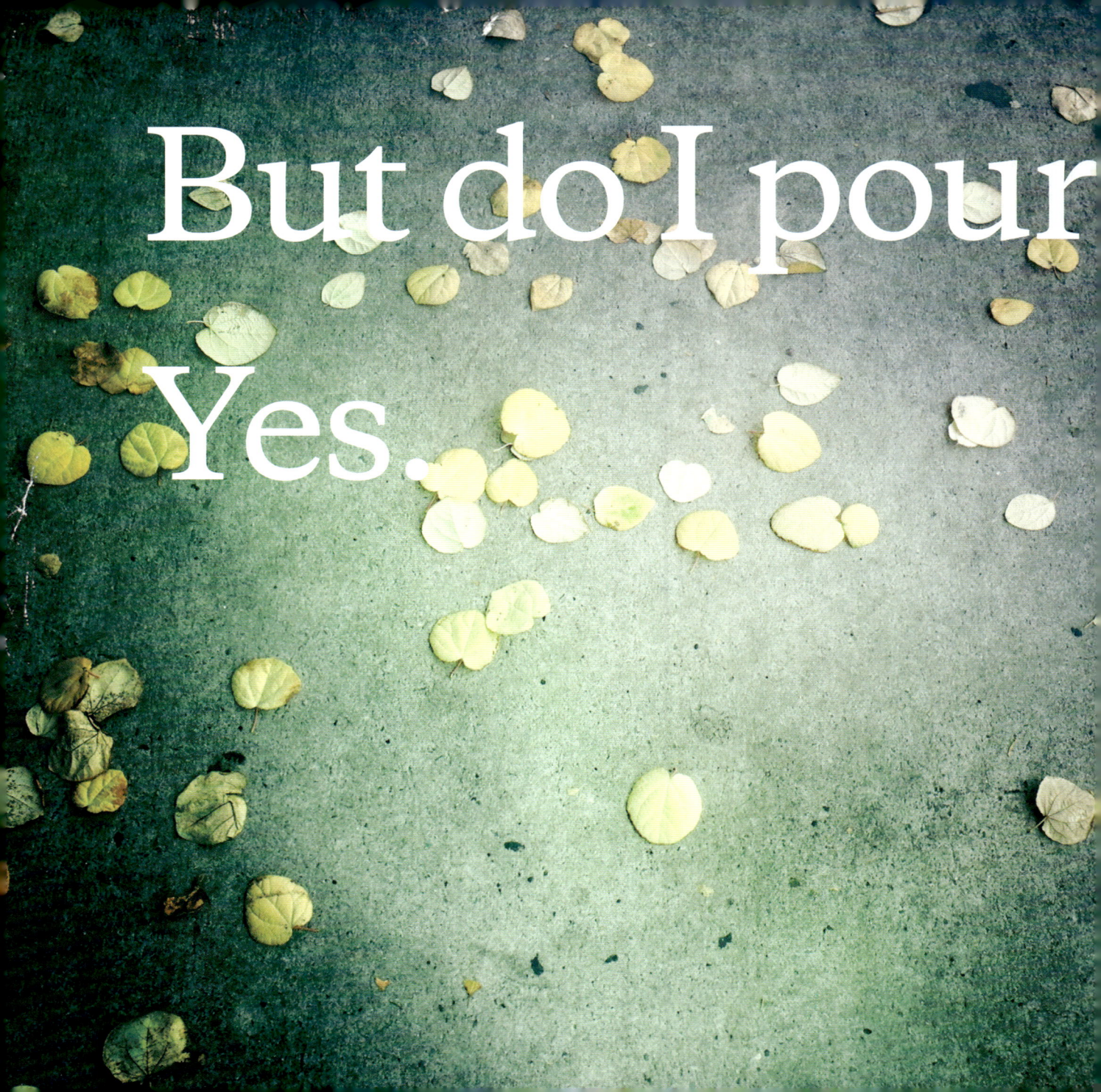

Concrete

In high school, I have an odd-jobs business
Mowing lawns, painting houses, moving families.
I do landscaping, build patios and decks, even clean windows
For the right price.

Basically, I'll do anything.
My method is, first get the job,
Then figure out how to do it.
There's a network of construction guys I can go to
For a quick lesson on whatever I've gotten myself into.
They get a kick out of my
Will-do-even-though-I-don't-know-how-to attitude.

One time, I get a contract to pour a driveway.
(Who hires a bunch of 17-year-old kids to pour concrete?)
I go see Larry, my friend Mark's dad.
He's a contractor, and one of the biggest, meanest dudes I know.
Larry shakes his head; he can't believe I'm going to try a driveway
But he lights up a cigarette and tells me how to do it anyway.

It works. The driveway gets done, and it looks pretty good.
Larry stops by during the day, and saves my ass at a key moment.
If he hadn't, I'd be breaking concrete for a week.
I get paid, though wind up not making much
Because I severely underestimate the time and materials needed for the job.
But do I pour the driveway? Yes.

Put that in the same column as
Writing a symphony,
Scoring contemporary dance works,
Sitting down with Bloods and Crips to write a song,
Writing a book.
Just because I don't know what I'm doing when I start
Doesn't mean that I don't make it happen.
I just need help.

> Be willing to fail and you just might win.
> We're capable of doing, of being, many things if we just say yes.
> Be brave enough (or dumb enough) to try.
> If you just get going, and keep your eyes open,
> You'll find the help you need.

But unless you know what you're doing,
Stay away from concrete work
Or get yourself a Larry.

3.
No Plan B
Commitment

Johnny's Song

Sing the blues for Baton Rouge
Just don't over do it
Johnny don't care
He ain't cutting his hair
And you know he can see right through it
                    –Johnny's Song

I don't really write that.
The words come through me fully formed,
Landing on my shoulder in the middle of the night,
Moving through my mind, my guitar, voice,
Pen to paper in my room the next day.

I know something is happening but can't name it.
It's new, but familiar somehow,
What I've been looking to reach, or get back to,
Like the first time I got high.

The song is better than my skills as a writer.
I'm just the wheel it is rolling on.
And I wonder, why me?
What did I do to deserve this bit of grace?
It's the first time I've had a song come this way.
I'm 17.

I play the song for my girlfriend.
She comes up to me at school the next day
And says, "Don't play that for anyone.
It'll freak them out.
The world's not ready for you."

That's when I know I'm onto something.
If a song coming through me
Makes her say that
Then I need to dive down that well every time,
Swim in that sea.
This song holds a truth and that's where I want to live.

Standing in the hallway by my locker,
Though I have no idea what it really means to do so,
That is the moment I commit myself to songs.

Needless to say, we break up soon after that.

Maui, 2017

A Hotel With a View of the Freeway

People are fascinated when I tell them I'm a songwriter, a musician.
That I tour here and there
And know a few famous people.

They see the bright lights, glamour
Maybe. Freedom, youth.
But what they don't see is the cost of this life,
What it takes to make it happen.

The time away from home, your kids,
An all-too-common instability,
Scratching for money, then
Hoarding it when it does come in.
With every album, every song and show
Hanging your soul in the wind
So some jerk with a pen who had a bad day
Can slap you down,
Making you doubt your own talent.
They don't see you get back up again,
Believing. Always believing.

It's impossible for them to sit beside you
In all the late-night hotel rooms
Staring out at the freeway
In San Diego, Atlanta, Munich
Wondering if you made the right call.

I'm not complaining
But let's be real.
There are times, sitting there in the quiet, alone
When I doubt my choices.

Before jumping into this life,
Know the struggle will come at you
In one form or another.
Get ready

For the most beautiful existence on the planet.

M4 at Night, 2009

Following spread:
Cigarette on a Taxi Floor, NYC, 2016,
Comb on a Sidewalk, Kansas City, 2017

Get in the Van

A friend in London says that
If you're not in the van by 23,
Driving across the country
Playing shows
For barely enough money
To pay the bills
And loving it,
You'll never make it in music.

It's hard work getting ready, getting good,
Building the foundation.
The hours alone, in your room
Listening, dreaming, practicing.
The miles on the highway,
Late nights, early mornings
Trying to finish a song
No one will hear.

Start early,
Do your homework
So that when the bright light finally hits you
You're ready.
You can handle it.

The Disappearing Pop Star

Everyone wants to be a rock star these days.
Kids see a TV show, write a couple of songs,
Play a few shows
And think they're ready.

It doesn't really happen like that.
And even if it did, you don't want that path.

Too-quick fame — that's a set-up
For the disappearing pop star.

It's thin. And when the success goes away
There's nothing to brace the fall,
No structure from which to rebuild.

Music Is a Blue-Collar Gig

Advice to parents whose kids want to be musicians:
Leave them alone.

Give them the space to practice, explore, imagine,
Get lost in the sound, the raw making of it.
Let them be that kid in the bedroom,
Staring at the posters,
Falling asleep with their guitar,
Listening.

Let them be frustrated.
They need to cultivate their own deep hunger
For music beyond all reason.
A drive for self-expression
That defies all the voices
Telling them to get real
And stop their dreaming.
They have to find something to say
That is uniquely theirs.

With love, let them lose.
With kindness, hurt a bit.
You'll be doing them a favor
That will pay off later on.

Music is a blue-collar gig.
Kids need to learn to carry their own amp,
The value of a good guitar,
How to get by with less
And finally win on their own
After coming up short more than a few times.

Charlie Sexton at the Piano, 2016

Sleeping on Couches

If you want to make a living with art, music
Or anything outside of the mainstream
That may require a bit of wandering,
Start young. It's easier to explore,
To pick up and follow a tangent,
When drifting isn't so expensive.

Once you get to be 40,
Making a wholesale tack
Toward a dream you let go of years ago
Can cause a lot of damage.
People start counting on you.
You've got responsibilities.

And it's a little too late to start
Sleeping on couches.

Couch, Austin, 2013

Following spread:
Flowers, London, 2017

With love, let
With kindness,
You'll be doing
That will pay

them lose.
hurt a bit.
them a favor
off later on.

Get in or Get Out

Bill Worrell and Spider Johnson, the first real working artists I ever meet, have me cornered in the kitchen at a party. I'm 23, a kid hanging with the older kids, trying to figure out how the music/art game works. They look me square in the eye and tell me, "Stop messing around. Get serious. Either commit to being an artist or quit. Because if you can't commit, if you can't give it your everything, it'll never work. It's too easy to bail."

They're right. I know it, and it scares the shit out of me.

The art life is just that — a life.
It's more than just a job.
Your days have to be built around it.
If you can't make that commitment,
You'll never survive.
You'll burn out and find a reason to stop.

Get in or get out.
Don't look back.

Bill Worrell's Hands, 2018

No Plan B

My first wife and I get engaged when I'm 22
And her father sends me the letter.
He's very concerned about my career choice
And wonders if I would consider a trade school;
Something to fall back on.

After I calm down, I write him a letter.
I tell him that my father always told me to never have a Plan B.
If you have it, you'll use it.

I also say that when I get to be 30, if there's absolutely zero chance
Of making a living at music,
Then I'll think about some other line of work.
But until then, no.

The marriage doesn't work out,
But the plan does.

By the way, I grew to love this guy, and he became a big fan. Word has it that when I got my first press in Chicago, he carried a copy of the story around to show his friends.

Motorcycle, 2014

Completely Unemployable

Boo Hewerdine and I sometimes talk about how amazing it would be to have a job —
Someone to tell us what to do, where we don't have to come up with all the ideas
And make sure the schedules and budgets work year after year. It's exhausting.

But the truth is that we're both completely unemployable in any traditional sense
And would last about a day and a half at a real job.
We'd be the one staring out the window, humming a tune
Thinking about nothing in particular.

Once you get far enough down the road of being an artist, you can't turn back.
But why would you?

That's when it starts to get really good.

Darden Smith and
Boo Hewerdine,
Halsway Manor, 2017

Welding

I'm thinking about quitting music.
It's the late '90s, and I have no work, not much money,
A 6-month-old daughter, a 5-year-old son,
And reality is having a hard time keeping up with the dream.
One project after another is falling through.
The calendar is full of empty pages.
I need some money, fast.
So I become a welder.

My friend Richard puts me to work at what he calls "career refocusing camp."
For the next six months, three days a week, I weld, hang gutters, dig ditches for pipe.
He pays me in cash.
I hide inside the dark green world of the welder's helmet,
Get lost in the routine, the smell of burning metal, earth, sweat.
But I know it won't last.

Late on a Friday afternoon,
I'm listening to Terry Gross interview Randy Newman on *Fresh Air*.
He talks about his work, all he's had to put up with in his years of doing music.
And it makes me realize that I have to either quit music
Or quit welding.
I can't do both.
If I stay at this for too long
I won't be able to pick up the guitar again.
I'll lose the momentum,
Drift too far away from music,
Too far from the commitment,
Too far from my joy.

I clean up the shop,
Put the tools away, sweep the floor, stack the scraps,
Walk in the office and tell Richard that I won't be back on Monday.
"It took you long enough," he says.

    Sometimes we have to go 180 degrees from our imagined destination
    To find which road we're supposed to follow,
    Where we can do the most good in the world.

    I could be a highly average welder
    Or one of a dozen other pursuits
    But that's not what I was put on the planet to do.
    It's not about working hard; for me, that's a given.
    Welding reminds me that I know how to work.

    The trick is to constantly be creating opportunities
    To live and work in that place where my curiosity and abilities intersect
    The collision point of passion, drive and talent
    And to keep putting my shoulder into that wheel.

Following spread:
Water Tanks, NYC, 2012

Process

There's no difference between
Writing a song,
Painting a picture,
Building a house,
Or cooking a meal for your family.
Every action can be a creative act
If you put yourself into it fully
And take the time to get it right.

The first step is making an agreement with yourself
To believe you can.
The art follows.

From Columbus Circle, 2016

Play Music First

When I get up in the morning,
I pick up a guitar as soon as I can.
If I'm at home, I might sit down at the piano.
Regardless, I play music first thing.

It wasn't always this way.
I used to wake up and start "getting things done."
Phone calls, errands, paperwork; the endless minutia of life.
But these actions, this busy-ness,
They just support my work.
They're not why I'm here.

Without songs, without music,
There is no reason for me to make phone calls.
There is no one to call.

Know what drives you,
And let that be your focus.
Drift too far from that compass point,
And one day you'll look up
To find yourself

Lost.

Gold, San Francisco, 2013

Practice

My friend Sammy Merendino is a drummer living in New York City. He's toured the world, played on hundreds of records, done Broadway, commercials, TV and film music ... you name it.

His playing, his time-keeping, is meticulous. He hits the drums hard, really driving a band. When he sits at a drum kit, he has an almost regal presence. Sammy belongs behind the drums.

I'm staying at his house in Harlem while working in the city for a few days. It's the spring of 2011 and he's supposed to be on a tour, but it's suddenly canceled. He has no work on the immediate horizon. Some people might worry. Sammy takes another tack.

Coming back to the house in the afternoon, as soon as I round the corner from Broadway onto 147th Street, I hear drums. Sammy's practicing. I stand on the sidewalk, listening to him work out a complicated double-bass drum pattern. Again and again he runs through it, till he gets it right.

Inside the house, I ask him how long he's been at it. "Four hours. I try to get in around five a day," he says.

Five hours a day. There's no specific reason for his practicing; he just wants to keep in shape, so that when the call does come, he's ready.

And that's why Sammy keeps working. Because he always wants to be better. Where others might coast, he pushes. It's the reason he's good.

Even when he doesn't have a gig, he practices.

Sammy Merendino, NYC, 2017

Scales and Demos

I meet Bob Glaub in 1987, when I'm out opening shows for Rodney Crowell. Bob is playing bass in Rodney's band. He's played on hundreds of recordings, including some of my favorites — albums by Jackson Browne and Warren Zevon that had a big impact on how I hear bass and drums — and he's a righteous guy, and a real gentleman to me on the tour.

After the last show, in Boston, he says that if I'm ever in L.A., I should come stay at his place. I'll have to sleep in the studio, but it's free. So of course I book writing trips out there just to hang out with Bob.

My first time there, he's showing me around the studio and I notice sheet music on a stand.
"What's that?" I ask.
"Oh, those are my practice charts. I come out here every day and warm up."
"Every day?"
"Every day."

"Oh, and I'll need to get in here tomorrow morning around 9 o'clock to get ready for a session," he says.
I'm thinking Linda Ronstadt, Stevie Nicks or some other big-time artist.
"Yeah? Who you working with?" I ask.
"I'm not sure. A friend is producing some demos for a new writer and called to see if I could play on them."
"You do demos?"
"Absolutely. You never know when some new kid is going to turn out to be the next Jackson Browne."

So here's Bob Glaub, star L.A. session player, doing demos for some unknown songwriter,
putting the same amount of attention and focus into this as he would an album for a big-time act.

Bob isn't caught up in the status. He just shows up and does the work.

Empire, 2017

Hunger

Nashville, 1996

Rodney Crowell is on his way to my hotel to pick me up for breakfast. I'm wondering why. We've toured together a few times and run into one another in airports and on New York street corners, but I don't know Rodney that well.

Like so many events in my life, I'm not sure how I got here, but here I am.

He shows up in a brand new Lexus. This is the first time I've been in one, maybe even seen one. "Nice ride," I say.

"Yeah," he says. "Pretty tall cotton." (That's one of my favorite Texas phrases.)
"You know, I've done well, but I never did so well that I wasn't hungry. I've always had to work."

"All my friends who don't have to work? Their songs start to suck," he notes. "They're not hungry anymore."

Considering Rodney's output, from songwriting, recording and touring to producing and writing books, it's clear he both wants to work, and needs to. What I love most about Rodney is that he never stops pushing himself, when others would just settle.

There are many ways to get paid.
Hunger comes in many forms.
Call it drive, desire, passion, the need to pay the bills; it's all the same.
It's that voice telling you to get busy, make something.
It's wanting be better, going a little deeper, constantly striving to find something new.

Rodney Crowell, 2016

Following spread:
Trellick Tower, London, 2012,
Midtown, NYC, 2014

Suffering for the Sake of Suffering

Suffering for the sake of suffering for your art is bullshit.
Life is already full of suffering.
Why add to it for the wrong reason?

Living for your art seems like a much better plan.

Black-Eyed Man, Paris, 2012

4. The Habit of Noticing
Presence

Wake Up

My first job is to wake up.
Every day.

To pay attention
And notice what is right
In front of me.

To practice seeing, hearing
What most people miss.

How can I translate the big picture
If I'm not tuned into
The smallest
Details?

*The Lobbyist, Hotel DuPont,
Washington, D.C., 2017*

This Is Not a Mistake

Every night onstage,
I look for that moment
When the guitar, the song,
Sound, the room, fall together
And the music swims.
Sometimes it happens only once.
Other nights, it comes on rapid-fire.
Occasionally, it's when I'm in the dressing room
Before the show,
Alone.

Even when no one is listening
Or the club is half-empty
On the worst of nights
I can still find these moments of complete perfection,
When I'm reminded that my whole life has brought me here

And that this is not a mistake.

Greg Trooper's Martin D35, 2017

The Habit of Noticing

On those days when I'm stuck in an airport
Or have a day off somewhere like Kansas City
Or find myself standing in London on a cold train platform,
I grab a pen and notebook
And draw the first thing I see.

It's all about the habit of noticing,
And then making something new.

Flight Delay, 2017

Following spread:
Ocotillo, 2017

Words Matter

Words matter.
What comes out of your mouth
Puts voice to what is moving through your mind,
Whether or not you like what it says.

Years ago, during a very difficult time,
I tell a friend that my life is "really fucked up."
He says I should watch my language.
Not because I shouldn't swear,
But just to be aware of what I'm saying.
The reality is that I'm going through a tough time.
If I want to say it's "fucked up," I can.
But at the moment, the situation isn't quite that bad.
If I keep phrasing it this way, I'll start to believe it.
The more I believe it, the closer it comes to being real
And that's not good.

When words are married to intentions
We have the ability to shift outcomes.

Words matter.
People are listening.
Be very clear about what you want,
What you're asking for.

When you use the right words, you just might get it.

Collaboration

When I make records, I rarely tell the musicians what to play.
I get the best players I can, and pay them as much as I can afford.
I want my money's worth, so first, I want to hear what they hear
Then build off that.
Their ideas are almost always better than mine.

Know what it is that only you can do.
Work with people who are different.
Allow yourself to be amazed
And be willing
To be wrong,

To not be the smartest person in the room.

Warren Barigian

I'm sitting in an Austin hotel suite in the middle of the afternoon, waiting for Warren Barigian. He's a voice coach. Very famous, apparently. He works with opera singers, rock stars. Meat Loaf.

Someone, I still don't know who, paid $750 for me to get this lesson.
That's a lot of money. This better be good.

Warren sits down and says, "So you're a singer? Good. Pick a phrase from any song and sing it to me 10 different ways."

No problem. I start singing the opening lines from "Skylark."

"Skylark, have you anything to say to me ..."
I get three passes in before he stops me.
"You're repeating yourself. I said to sing each one different. Try it again."

I start once more. After a couple of tries, same thing,
"You're repeating yourself. Do it again. Don't think about it."

We do this dance three or four more times before he throws up his hands.
"Stop worrying about the notes and just sing it! Every time you repeat yourself, you cut off your creativity."

Then he turns around and walks out of the room. The lesson is over.

I sit there for a few minutes, trying to figure out what just happened. Only later, after I put a few days between us, does it settle in my mind and start to make some sense.

My voice isn't perfect, and never will be. But the way I sing, the reason, the person behind the notes, Warren changes all that.

Twenty years later, I still think about the lesson, about not repeating myself. Ever.

Here's the deal: No matter what you're doing, do it like there's no tomorrow, as if this is the first time and last time. Everything depends on *now*.
When you sing, sing in that moment.

When I think about it that way, $750 is cheap.

Now, 2014

The House Manager

I'm in Newcastle, England, playing a small, old-fashioned theater complete with a backstage full of sets and wardrobes from forgotten plays. It's dusty, cramped. To find the bathroom, I have to wind through what feels like a maze.

The house manager, a funny little guy about 70 years old, calls lighting cues from a chair beside the stage. He's like countless other house managers across the globe. The shows come and go. He's at his table, watching from the wings as the drama unfolds under his lights.

This is his world. I'm just dropping in for the night.

Before I go onstage, I take a look at his station. A hundred stories hide among the notes, photos, notices and reviews taped to the wall. Yesterday's newspaper sits on the floor. An empty ashtray rests on the table.

He knows nothing about me, has never heard my music. When I'm onstage, I look over and see him at his post. He's watching me, listening. There's an audience out there in front of me, yes, but I realize halfway through my set that really, I'm playing only to him. All I care about is, "Is he listening?"

For some reason I want him to remember this moment, if only for an hour or so. I want him to go home thinking about something that happens on this stage tonight; some line from a song, something I say.

After the show, as I'm wrapping my cables and putting my guitars away, he comes up to me and says that he likes my songs, and the stories in-between. They remind him of a play.

I go back to the horrible little hotel where I'm staying, satisfied that I connected with my audience tonight: the house manager.

Every show has a different soul.
You have to sing to it.

Newcastle, 2016

Everything

I have been to London, and I've been to New York
I had some damn fine wine, good food upon my fork
Still there is a hunger that won't go away
I long to feel the beauty in every day
Yeah I want it all, everything
All the joy that life can bring
When I'm gone here's a song
I hope to hear you sing
He wanted it all
Everything

Hawk upon the wing, horses on the run
A wave upon the ocean, my daughter and my son
And when I'm still aching after all of this
I want my love to take me with a kiss
Yeah, I want it all, I want everything
All the joy that love can bring
When I'm gone here's a song
I hope to hear her sing
He wanted it all
Everything

I don't need to hold it
That's not the way to live
I just want to have it all
So I can give it all away
Give it all away

Yeah, I want it all, I want everything
All the bounty this life can bring
And when I'm gone here's a song
I hope the angels sing
He wanted it all
Everything
Yeah, 'cause I want it all
Everything

Flatiron, 2017

"Everything," from the 2017 album of the same name.

5.
Do What You Do, Kid
Authenticity

Do What You Do, Kid

1993

It's Columbia Records night at a convention sponsored by the Musicland record-store chain. The lineup is Tower of Power, Tony Bennett and me. I'm first, of course. My record, *Little Victories*, just came out. After my set, I tell one of the Columbia marketing guys that I must meet Tony. It's important. When will I ever get this chance again? Thirty minutes later, I'm escorted into his dressing room, introduced as "a new artist on the label."

He says, "I remember when I was new on the label. That first year, I had four songs in the top 20 at the same time." (I'm thinking, "What? Four at the same time?") There's a group of us, but he turns to look straight at me, and says, "But it all went away. Gone. Poof! I was nothing. Then I had 'I Left My Heart in San Francisco.' I was back on top. But then it all went away again! Believe me, when it went away that time, kid, it went far, far away. Nobody wanted to hear from Tony Bennett. I could barely get work in America. Ralph [Sharon, his longtime piano player] and I would travel the world, just the two of us, playing little clubs, cruise ships, some of the rooms so small we didn't even use a PA! Remember that, Ralph?"

Ralph nods.

"That's when I started painting. I was in these places sometimes for a week, two weeks at a time, bored out of my mind, so I started painting. That went pretty well, though. For a while, I made more money painting than I did singing."

He breaks into a big smile, puts his arms out, and says, "And now it's back! Better than ever!"

He chuckles, takes my face in his hands, gives me an old-school cheek pat and says, "Do what you do, kid. If it's gonna be big, it'll be big. But always do your thing your way. I never did disco. Never. Just do what you do."

Then he walks out of the dressing room and onto the stage.

We're here for a reason. Know who you are and what you stand for. If you fail, go out swinging for your truth. There's nothing more hollow than success at something you don't believe.

Whenever I doubt my direction, or think my career might have turned out differently had I changed my style, I remember Tony.

Do what you do, kid.

Swimming

I'm swimming, staring at the bottom of the pool
Thinking about my work,
All the directions I want to go,
The reasons I can't stay on the same track
That has carried me for the last 20 years.
It hits me that I'm not really in the music business anymore.
I'm in the Darden Smith business.

Music is still in everything I do
But now there's teaching, writing, speaking,
SongwritingWith:Soldiers
Along with the albums and shows.
It all comes from the same internal fire,
Except it's different now
And the old label seems like a straitjacket.

If I just stay true to this business of being myself,
Honest to all that I am,
I realize, it can get really good.

It's so simple, so obvious
That I start laughing
Face down in the water
And damned near drown.

Following spread:
Heathrow in the Rain, 2016

what we're supposed to be

we really are.

Lists

She asks me to tell her 10 things, in order,
That I want to accomplish with my work.

I do, and then she has me write them down.
When I do that, the list flips.

What was number 10 on the first list is number 1 on the second.
Where touring was at the top before, now it's way down the line.
Writing, teaching — these things rise up.

She asks, "Which one is true?"

Sometimes our image of what we're supposed to be
Gets in the way of what we really are.

I remember the first list
And follow the second.

Shadow, NYC, 2016

The Truth of Jean Cocteau

Joe Ely says that before he starts a new project,
Like a book or a record, he takes a trip up above the Caprock
To the plateau around Lubbock and Amarillo.
The Texas Panhandle.
He needs to see the sky, feel the wind.

Lyle Lovett tells me that he often feels like
His back is against a wall and he's looking out,
Comparing everything in the world to Houston.

I hear that Jean Cocteau once told Man Ray
To never completely sever
His American roots
Because that is the source of his art.

Know where you come from.
Have a perspective, a point of view.
Always remember what it is and how to find it.

Lyle Lovett, 2018

Background Noise

My job is to be true,
To see, and say, what is really there.
Everything else is just background noise.

Don't shy away from crisis
Or hide from difficult days,
But use them to mine the world.
I think that's the whole point of this life —
To seek out a perspective that's yours alone,
Carved from all you see and hear,
Revel and struggle through.
To go into the wilderness and bring back
The diamond

That only you can find.

Trans Pecos at High Speed, 2018

An Artist's Guide to Fashion

What you wear doesn't matter
As long as you look like you know you put it on.

Beauty, Paris, 2013

Bells and Whistles

Los Angeles, 1987

Marty Lewis, who worked on some of the great Jimmy Buffett and Dan Fogelberg records, is mixing my first album for CBS/Epic. He's a big deal — at least, he seems like one to me. I feel like a punk kid next to this guy, and don't know what to do, so I just hang around the studio trying not to get in the way.

When a new mix is ready, Marty turns up the volume, then he and I go sit in the lounge next to the control room to listen and make notes. It's bizarre that there are all these big speakers in the other room, but we make our decisions out by the coffee maker.

One day, he says, "Remember, the most important part of a record is the song. If you don't have that, all this studio stuff is just bells and whistles. It's the cheapest part as well. It doesn't cost money to write the song. Too many people throw good money at crap songs."

He pauses for a minute to let that sink in, then stands and walks back into the control room to set up the next mix, saying,

"It's like building a house. Start with a good foundation, and the rest is easy."

Spin

My friend Rob starts a coffee-roasting business.
As soon as his friends hear about it, they start asking how
He's going to spin the marketing.

He tells me this over an espresso,
Looking at me and saying,
"How about we roast really good coffee.
Then we'll worry about the spin.
Because if we get that first part wrong,
It'll never work and
The spin is just bullshit."

Following spread:
Grass, Colorado, 2017,
Dry Tree, Texas, 2018

First You Have to Take Good Pictures

If you ask photographer Michael O'Brien
How he got all his great photo assignments,

He'll tell you that first
You have to take good pictures.

There's no hidden angle.
No secret way through the door.

Michael O'Brien, 2018

D.L. Cerney

In New York City there is a little clothing store, D.L. Cerney.
I like to go there when I'm in town, run my hands across the fabric, try on the shirts.

Aside from the clothes, it's Duane, the D in D.L., who keeps me coming back. Many times, it's just the two of us, talking cotton and gabardine, buttons, the lineage of the design, the craft.

I know of other places like this, where I go not only for what they're selling, but for the people who run the shop, the stories of what they've seen; I go to hear them talk about what they do. In London, behind Kensington Church, there's a little store called Hornets that has the same allure; it's like a salon or clubhouse.

What draws me to D.L. Cerney is the meaning and passion that wraps around the experience of the clothes. The commerce seems almost an afterthought. In his look, the way he greets me, how he stops for conversation, his commitment to not only the clothes, but their making, the way they're tried on, their look and feel, it's evident that Duane cares deeply. He invites you in. I think I buy so many of those damned shirts because I just like being around Duane.

Fall in love with what you do.
It's infectious.

Shirt, 2016

Perfection Is Boring

When I draw, I try to put on paper what I see.
Some reflection of the thing that caught my eye.
I couldn't draw a straight line if I had to,
But that's not the point.
Perfection is boring.

I'm not really interested in reproducing exactly what is there.
We already have that.

Make something new.
Don't worry about getting it perfect.
Get it right.

Under the Monkey Pod, 2018

Following spread:
Monument Valley, 2015

Being bored with your life

is the worst. Don't allow it.

The Edge

1.
There's a place where you feel most on fire, most at home.
Some call it bliss; the zone. Flow.
I call it the edge.

It's a way of living.

For me, it centers on music, songs and art.
But it's also in the connections: family, beauty, writing,
Travel, the people, the planning,
All my daydreams.

I find it when I'm moving at top speed, juggling multiple things, laughing.
It's there at the end of the day, in the stillness,
Knowing that my time was well spent.

It's important to identify and pursue your own edge,
Not some imitation or replica that merely looks enticing.
It'll be different than mine
And no doubt will change with the years.
It's vital to keep looking, finding, losing,
Then finding it again.

Every day you wake up and your mind hums with opportunity,
Your joy flows out of your actions, your work.
They all crash into each other, igniting the best
And the separation dissolves.

2.
Just so you know,
Feeling alive can be addicting.
It's difficult, at times even a burden, to always be searching for the edge.
Chasing it can wear you out.
But what a way to go.

3.
To me, it looks like this:

At the angle, on the edge of the cliff — that's the place where you are most alive. It's where you lose track of time, where your actions and efforts line up with your dreams and abilities. You're fully engaged, fully aware, vulnerable. There's skin in the game.

That's where you want to be.

This is not about acting dangerously, or throwing everything away in pursuit of a crazy dream. It's not a choice between having — or not having — money or things. It's about being the person you are supposed to be, doing the work that you love.

Below the cliff is what I call "the Valley of Golden Opportunity." It's the great unknown, the place of possibility. All that might be.

A move away from the edge is a lean toward safety, security — a move you make out of fear, or maybe a misguided feeling of responsibility or expectation. You can certainly go in this direction, and you might have what seems to be a very successful life. But inside, something is missing; you feel a certain hollowness. You can build a big house, but even if you crawl onto the roof, you still can't see the whole valley. To see everything, you have to go to the edge. And the farther you move away from that view, the more distance you put between you and your best, most alive self.

4.
As I get older,
I come across a lot of people
Who miss that feeling of being alive; on fire.
The problem is that, with each passing year
It gets a little more difficult to get back there.
Change gets expensive with age.

I've known more than a few relatively sane adults who
In a mad dash for the edge
Lose their bearings and go off the cliff.

We need both: opportunity and safety.
One without the other isn't healthy.

But being bored with your life is the worst. Don't allow it.

Plug in.

The sooner you can find what lights you up, the better.
Live as close to that edge as possible.

6.
I'll See Your Talent and Raise You a Phone Call
Endurance

The Teasers

As a kid, I like to draw pictures.
But being left-handed, stuck in those damned right-handed desks at school,
I have a hard time making drawings that aren't lopsided and weird.
The other kids, being kids, tease me about the bizarre scrawls on my paper.
So at the bitter age of 10, I figure out how to make the teasing stop:
I quit drawing.

I make up a story,
And the story is, "I can't draw."

In 1989, I'm in L.A. recording what will become *Trouble No More*.
Sitting in the studio, bored, scratching on a newspaper with a pencil,
I accidentally draw a tree.
Immediately, I cover the drawing up, afraid someone will see it.
A few seconds later, I move my hand. It's still there.
Suddenly I'm 9, sitting in the back of the class,
Lost in the land of crayons and construction paper.
It feels good. I start to teach myself to draw again.

Now when I travel, I fill notebooks with weird little black-and-white pictures.
There's not a straight line to be found, and it doesn't matter.
I don't make these images to show people.
I don't need a gallery wall for proof they're valid.
The doing of it is all that matters now.

Sometimes I think about all those years I spend believing that story
I tell myself when I'm 10: the story of no.

Because I listen back then, I miss out on a lot of joy,
A lot of time dragging ink across a page.

Don't listen to the teasers.
Draw the pictures.

Girl With an Umbrella, 2016

Reviews

1987

We're somewhere in Canada. Edmonton maybe. Or Calgary.
I'm in the dressing room, waiting to open for Emmylou Harris,
Reading a review of my record in the local paper.
It's not good.
I'm shattered.

Later, Emmylou says,
"Don't read your reviews.
If they're good, you'll believe it; it'll go to your head.
If they're bad, they'll ruin your day."

I've always kept this advice close.

Reviews are just someone's opinion.
They have zero to do with anything real.
Thumbs up, thumbs down; neither are completely true.

Don't put yourself through the turmoil.
Very few egos can handle the good or the bad.
Just do your work; don't let the chatter get stuck in your mind.

River From a Plane, 2017

It's Not the Magna Carta

David Kahne is the head of A&R at Columbia Records in the early '90s. I'm in his office, waiting to play him some new songs. Some artists struggle with David, but we get along. He's straight with me, saying exactly how he feels about my stuff and listening when I have something to say. I love our meetings in his office. He has a piano in there. We sit around talking about music, listening to demos, coming up with song hooks ... David can actually play. He writes music, produces records. Odd as it may sound, an A&R man who plays an instrument is a rarity at a major record label.

On his walls hang pictures of ballerinas and a periodic table. Not a single shot of him with a pop star.

He finally walks in, throws his jacket on a chair, shakes his head and says, "Sorry I'm late. I was at the studio with an *artiste* and her people." He steps to the window, looks out at midtown Manhattan, and says, "Some of these people around here think way too much of themselves."

"What do you mean?" I respond.

"It's just a record. We make pop records. It's not the Magna Carta. Nobody's curing cancer here. People should remember that."

It's OK to be serious about your work,
But don't take yourself too seriously.
It's highly unattractive.

Cha Cha Mambo, 2018

Stage Fright

Everyone has bad days at work.
If you're a performer, those moments happen in the spotlight.
It's humiliating, but normal.

I start to conquer my stage fright when I realize that
No matter how prepared I am, I still make a lot of mistakes.
It's not a question of will I, but when will I mess up a song.

I laugh. Keep going.
My blunders become part of the show.

The audience usually doesn't know the difference.

Enchanted Rock, 2018

It'll Get Better

Vancouver, 1987

I want to disappear.
It's the first night of a three-week run
Opening for Emmylou Harris across Canada.
The theater holds about 2,500 seats.
Until now, the largest crowd I've played to is maybe 100 people.

My set does not go well.
After my last song, the applause stops
Before I can even put my guitar on the stand.

Walking offstage, I look up.
Emmylou is standing directly in front of me,
Just behind the curtain.
There's no way around;
I can't avoid her.
I'm going to have to say something,
But all that comes to mind is,
"That was terrible. I know it. I'll be leaving now ... thank-you."

But she's smiling, looking angelic in the backstage light.
Before I can say anything, she just puts a hand on my shoulder and says,
"Don't worry. It'll get better."

In that one sentence,
She acknowledges that yes, my set was bad.
But most important, she makes sure that I know
It happens to everyone.
She's had those nights, too.

She knows I bombed onstage
But has the kindness of spirit to speak to me,
Encourage me,
And keep me on the tour.
Some wouldn't have been so generous.

Emmylou is the first truly famous person I ever meet
And she shows me the value of being gracious on the way up,
At the peak, on the other side.

It lasts longer, and says more
Than any applause.

Following spread:
Windmill, Texas, 2013,
London Eye From a Cab, 2009

Eventually, the

Even if No One Hears It

It never ceases to amaze me how songs happen.
An idea sticks in my mind, words fall into shape,
A melody arrives out of nowhere,
And there's a new song from nothing.

Whenever I write a song, I say thanks,
Grateful that I was lucky enough to start
And then finish, one more.

Even if no one hears it.

Because every song is a blessing.
Even the ones that miss the mark,
Don't make sense,
Are boring or self-indulgent,
They're all worth writing

If only to get to the next one.

Fear of Not Being Brilliant

I think writer's block is mostly about fear.
Fear of not being brilliant.

Just start writing. Again.
It's better to scribble nonsense
Than to stare at blank paper.

If the words aren't any good
You can always keep them to yourself.
Or throw them away.

Eventually, the magic will return.

The Water Tap

My friend Gary Nicholson says he rarely gets writer's block.
To him, it's like a water tap.
If you turn it on every day, the tap works easily.
The water comes out clear.
Let it go a while — say, a couple of months,
Rust sets in and the water runs brown.
It takes a while before it runs clean.

Make something every day.
Turn the water on.

There's a confidence that comes
From believing that when you turn that handle,
Something good is going to happen.

Gary Nicholson, 2017

Boredom

My one fear in life is boredom.

If I ever get to a place
Where I feel stuck as an artist
And I don't try to fight my way out,
I need to stop.

The game is done.

Holland Tunnel, 2016

Boxes

Put yourself in a box, no matter how big
And eventually you will feel trapped.

Knock down the walls as soon as possible.
Repeatedly.

Gas Station, South Texas, 2017

Following spread
(Clockwise from top left): Barista, Swimmer, Danger-Dad, Breakfast, Towel, Poolside, Hair, Here's Another Thing, 2018

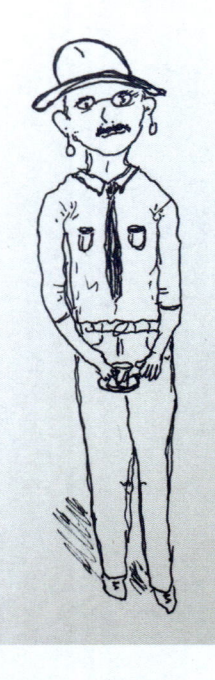

I'll See Your Talent and Raise You a Phone Call

2006

Why do some artists and musicians last
And others fall away, get out of the game?
Radney Foster and I are drinking whiskey,
Talking about what it takes to keep going in the music business.

At some point, everybody's good.
Big deal, you're talented.
What else you got?

What we came to is that it's the people
Who treat it like a job — they're the ones who last.
It's not a whim. They get serious.

Anybody who is half-good can get lucky once.
But when it happens over and over, it's not just luck.
There's something else.

I look over at Radney and say,
"I'll see your talent and raise you a phone call."

Jack Ingram and
Radney Foster,
Fredericksburg, Texas, 2016

Radney is from Del Rio, Texas, and you can tell it in the way he talks, his stride, the way his jeans fit over his boots. He's one of the hardest-working people I know, completely dedicated to making a living with music. Along with being one of my best friends and teachers, he is also a badass songwriter, singer, producer and chef.
And he does like his brown liquor, which I view generally as a positive thing.

Never Buy a Bus

1987

My piece-of-shit tour bus is parked at a diesel mechanic's outside of Austin.
I can't afford to fix it, and it's too broken to sell.
I'm wondering, "What was I thinking, buying this thing?"

Before I own it, the bus belongs to the Fabulous Thunderbirds.
Prior to that, Commander Cody and His Lost Planet Airmen.
And before they get it, it's a Brooklyn street bus.

Even when I'm first considering the deal,
Listening to Ray Benson
Try to talk me into buying it from the T-birds' Fran Christina,
All my instincts tell me to walk away.
But do I listen? Of course not.

What do I know? Maybe this is what you do when you get a record deal.
You buy a bus; go on the road.

But now I'm 27 years old, in debt,
Doing shows to support a bus that I didn't want in the first place.
Standing in that caliche parking lot, surrounded by big, broken machines,
I realize that I hate this bus. I have to ditch it.

A week later, I walk into Ray's office
And put the payment coupons and title on his desk.
"You want a bus?" I ask.

I just give it to him.
Sign it over and walk out the door.
It feels great.
All in all, I lose about $15,000 on the deal.
Considering what I learn, it's some of the best money I ever spend.

No. 1: Trust your instincts. Creative decisions, business decisions, love ... there's no difference. What might make sense for someone else could be a disaster for you. You already know the right choice. Don't talk yourself into a mistake.

No. 2: Never buy anything that you can't or don't want to maintain.

No. 3: If both Ray Benson and Fran Christina EVER try to convince you to do something, don't do it.

Fran Christina and Ray Benson are two of my favorite people in the world. Fran left the music business years ago and moved to Marfa, Texas, with his wife, Julie Speed. Ray still travels and plays with Asleep at the Wheel, the best damned western swing band in the world.

Luggage

My dad and I are watching TV
On a Saturday evening in 1978 and
One of the O.J. Simpson ads for Hertz rental cars comes on
Where he's running through the airport,
Jumping over furniture, spinning,
Moving fast.

Never taking his eyes off the screen, my dad says,
"You know why O.J. is able to move so fast there, son?
He doesn't have any luggage."

My dad is a mortgage guy.
Most of his stories end with a money moral.
His job is to help people get loans
To buy houses and cars.
He knows what it looks like
When people have too much debt,
Weighed down, stuck,
Focused on what's behind them
When all their dreams are out in front,
On the horizon.

The ability to explore, create, try new things
Is harder when you have debt leaning down on you.
You might want to stay out from under it as much as possible.

There's nothing that will slow you down
Like too much luggage.

Luggage, 2012

Following spread:
Red Beach 1 and 2, 2017/2018

You Can't Eat an Art Burger

Making money is rarely my main goal
And on occasion, this lands me in a serious bind.
I get swept up in the experience, the possibility of the work
And I forget about paying the bills.
I have to remember that I need both: money and the moment.

When I think about a project,
How I'm going to spend my time and energy,
It has to fill me up, and push me forward.
Money often becomes a distant concern.

The secret is in the balance,
Saying "yes" in the right degree.
There are many ways to get paid.
But it's good to remember that you can't eat an art burger.

Value

A DJ friend of mine tells me he's tired of club owners
Treating him like he's just another hired hand,
Just part of the scenery.
Disposable.

I tell him to double his fee.
He might work less in the short run,
But he'll make better money when he does
And not lose his spark in the process.
Even if he works half as much,
He'll still make the same money he is now
So what does he have to lose?

He does it,
And the first few months are kind of scary.
He loses a few gigs
With owners who don't want to pay him what he's worth anyway.

But in time, he has more work than ever
For more money.

> Too many artists get sucked into the idea that they aren't worth much,
> That if they're not scratching for a living, they're not valid.
> Out of some misguided fear that the work will dry up,
> We take any we can find, at any price.
>
> Flip it around.
> Work for people who respect what you do.
> When you show up, burn.
> Give them more than their money's worth
> Every time.
>
> Raise the bar.
> If you don't believe in the value of your work,
> Why should anyone else?

Grand Canyon

Perseverance is a good thing.
There's a lot to be said for grabbing onto an idea and clinging to it no matter what comes.

But sticking to some vision of what you think is supposed to happen — or worse, what you think you deserve — or being stubborn for the sake of proving a point while everything goes to hell around you ... not so good.

I remember being 23, playing at the bar in the lodge on the South Rim of the Grand Canyon. The gig is terrible — seven nights in a row — and I hate it. The tourists just want to hear Kenny Rogers songs. The saving grace is getting to hike the canyon. On a trail one day, I notice that the wind is moving bits of sand on what looks to be a solid rock wall. It's being rearranged, slowly, all around me, every second, forever.

Years later, when I'm around 40 and feeling caught between burnout, boredom and the need to make a living, the image of that sand comes to mind.

If the Grand Canyon can change, then surely I can.

Past Present Future, 2015

Finding the New Hat

Eventually, reinvention is a necessity for all of us.
It's one thing to be successful once,
But something entirely different to be able to make
Yourself over, to keep fresh
And continually find a new reason to keep moving.
The bottom will fall out at some point.
You'll be left with the remnants of a structure, a pattern that used to work.
You have to believe that something new will come
And all your wandering has a purpose.

You not only have to pull rabbits out of hats,
But some days, you have to wake up and go find whole a new hat.

Jardin du Luxembourg, Paris, 2013

Following spread:
Train Station, 2016

The Seven-Year Wave

1.
I ride a seven-year wave,
Ages 21 and 28, on through to 49 and now 56.
Rising and falling between clarity and deep confusion,
I repeatedly come up against myself,
The patterns I desperately need to break,
And the lessons there to be learned.

When I'm up, it feels like I'm absolutely where I belong.
At the bottom, I hit a wall, lost.
The ground shifts, and I have to adjust.
What has been working, doesn't.
Stagnation sets in
And I crave something new.

At this point, if I forget the central driver of who I am, what I do best,
I risk getting lost in doubt and second-guessing.
And the temptation is
To grasp for something, anything, to get back to the top.
In the past, I'd reach for shiny objects,
A quick fix, a side-show distraction
That would only cause great pain to those around me.

2.
It seems that when we're the most
Desperate for meaning is when
We most risk going off the rails.

But it doesn't have to be a disaster.
The lowest ebb can be a beautiful invitation
To reassess, to change.
A dry spell is the best time to look around,
Keep what works; get rid of the rest.

When you're on top, notice.
Ask why.
What about this time is right?
Which parts bring you joy?

Build on that.

3.
It's possible to jump out of the way once, twice even,
Put the reckoning off for another few years,
But eventually, it finds me.
And each time I sidestep the message,
Postpone the moment of clarity,
It just guarantees that the price, the pain, increases,
Until it's too late to do much but crash and
Hope for another chance.

4.
I know that the wave
Would be a lot easier to handle if I could
Turn my head away and
Sleepwalk through the struggle.

But if I did that, I'd miss the beauty of the high,
The lesson of the low.

Clocking this life
In all its pain and grace,
Noticing its rise and fall,
Is at the core of what I do:
Translating that experience
Into melody and words.

When I'm at the lowest point on the curve,
When I think the days couldn't get worse and
I wonder where I've mislaid my magic,
Song is still the only thing that
Consistently keeps me upright
On this beautiful
Ground.

5.
Step into the challenge of who you are,
The quicker, the better.
We hit bottom for a reason.
Pay attention.

Keep going.
There's beauty waiting for you
On top of the next wave.

Leonard Cohen's Coffee Table, 2017

7.
Echo
Meaning

Echo

We go about our day
Often thinking we have no effect,
No impact.
We stop here, go there.
While the truth is,
We don't see what happens in our wake.

When I'm on a plane, I like the window seat.
I look down at the cars, houses,
Spider-web subdivisions and freeways
Thinking there might be some
Kid in a backyard looking up
At that plane.

While back on the ground, I see a jet plume,
The silent glint of a plane out in front.
Someone's up there.
Maybe they're looking down at where I stand.

A plane casts a shadow.
A swimming pool reflects the sun.
You never know who is watching,
Listening for the echo of your voice.

From the Window Seat, 2017

The Deal

If it's possible to
Build your days around
What you love,
And you choose not to,
This is tantamount to a crime
Against us all.

Someone, somewhere in the world
Needs you to do this work,
To spend the time, write the song,
To break the code.

You may never meet them
But that doesn't lessen your value.

So please don't blow it.
A great deal is at stake.

Sunday Papers, London, 2017

Art at All Costs

Songwriter/photographer/architect Butch Hancock says, "Art at all costs."

That doesn't mean you have to be poor,
Living in some broken-down house.
You don't have to abandon all reason
So you can call yourself an artist.

But if you are a writer, write; a painter, paint.
If you're a parent, parent your children.

Just engage, completely.

Butch Hancock, 2015

Robert Henri

In his book, *The Art Spirit*,
American painter and teacher Robert Henri lays it out clearly:
The artist's life is beautiful,
But there's a price.

You do without.
It's hard on relations.
There is an extremely high failure rate.
You may wind up poor.
Forgotten.

But if you're willing to take that risk,
To make a life where your bills are paid from your creativity,
There's no better way to live.

You will be the envy of those who possess more
But whose work doesn't satisfy.

Don't go down this road unless you're ready to take that chance,
To pay that price.

Just know that if you do, and it works,
You will be paid in ways you never dreamed possible.

Scorpion, 2017

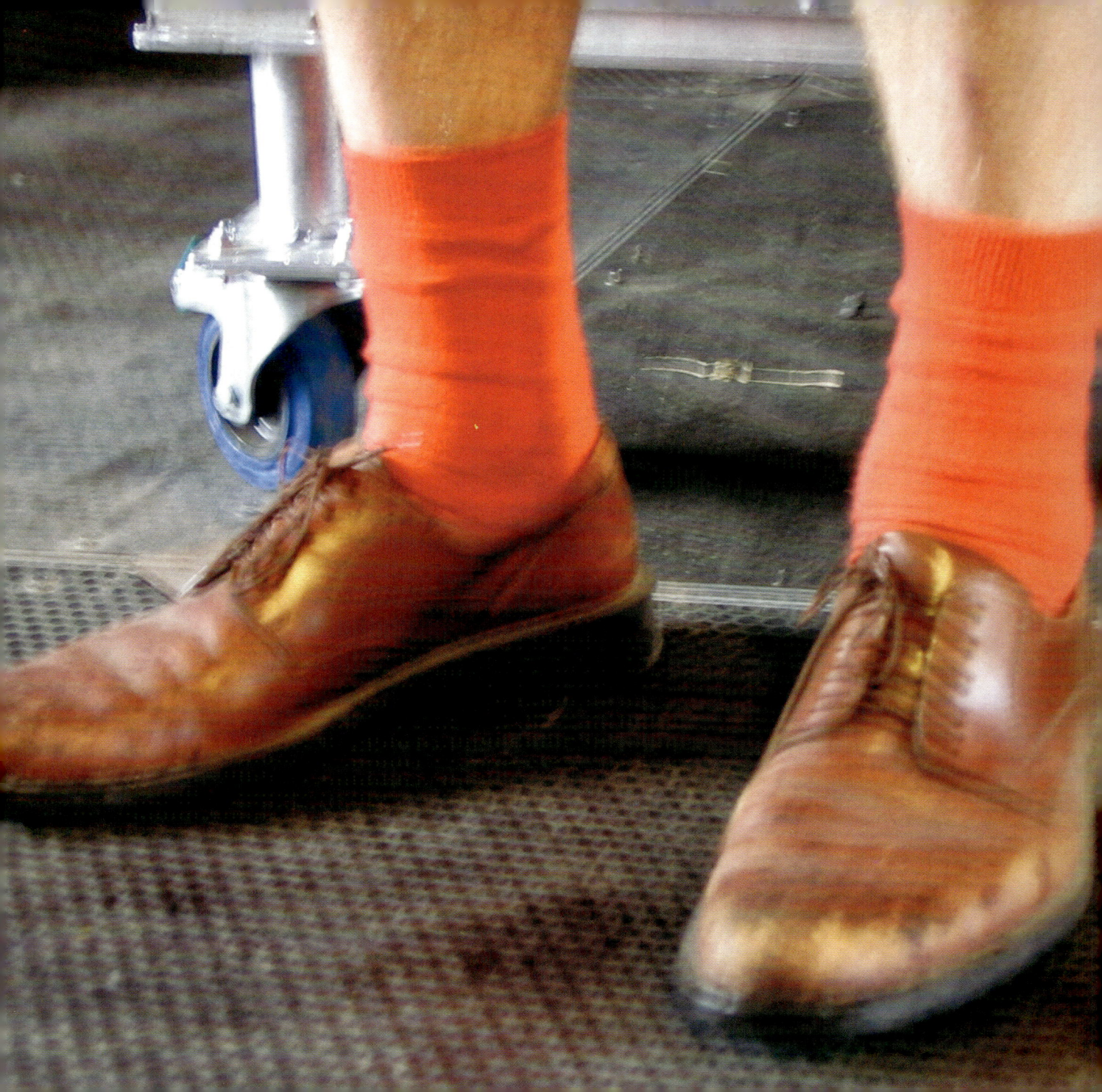

Lifestyle

There's no substitute for cash.

But over the course of my work I'm paid in lifestyle as much as anything.
Being able to spend my years doing what I love
And experiencing all I see out traveling —
These are luxuries never to be taken lightly.

Yes, there are rough times.
I don't have the stability (and bank accounts)
That some of my friends have — the ones with regular jobs.
My children grow up without the proverbial big-screen TV
But I don't think they're unduly scarred.
It's a sacrifice worth making.

And I would do it again.

Loudon Wainwright's Socks,
Ireland, 2012

My Real Work

I have an image, a snapshot of a moment
From almost every show I've ever played
When everything is lined up
And no single part could be better.
It has nothing to do with the crowd, the room,
The money, where I've been or where I'm going.
It's just pure
Now.

I live for these moments
And in many ways, play music
Because it's how I slip through
The tiny cracks in the mundane
And if only for a second, fly.

But these flashes, these glimpses of absolute joy
Are always there, all around me
As I move through the days and nights.

It's up to me to be ready
For the moments that come outside of music.

Being on the lookout —
This is my real work.

Rastas, Maida Vale,
London, 2016

An Afternoon With Paul Williams

Paul Williams is sitting next to me at a dinner in L.A.
His stories are hilarious.
He tells me how much fun he's having of late,
That after not writing songs for many years
He's only recently getting back into it.

I say, "Well, we should get together and write something."
He turns to me and says, "Really? What are you doing tomorrow?"

So here I am, spending an afternoon
Writing with Mr. Paul Williams,
And though our song is awful, completely forgettable,
The day is amazing.

As we work, he talks about his early days in Los Angeles, writing for everyone
From Three Dog Night and the Carpenters to the Osmonds,
Being on movie sets with Barbra Streisand,
The alcohol and drugs, the entire years lost and
How he eventually flames out,
Only to get sober and
Devote his time to helping others do the same.

"And now," he says, "I'm writing again. I'm so lucky."

At one point, while we're in the middle of figuring out the bridge, Paul jumps up and says, "God, I love writing songs. Don't you?"

I leave the session with something better than a song.
Paul Williams gives me a master class on life,
A map of where I want to wind up.
He doesn't really teach me anything about songwriting
But he shows me what it's like
To be truly excited
About the process.
How to disconnect,
Re-engage, and ignite again
After watching it all
Fall away.

Paul Williams, NYC, 2018

Following spread:
Fireworks on the Beach, 2014

The Party

I often have a party on December 26th
For my musician friends
And those around the edge
Photographers, designers, a sound engineer or two, a bartender.

The only caveat of attending is that
If you sing, then you have to give us a song.
Sit down with a guitar or at the piano
And play us something you love.
We rarely get the chance
To play just for each other
With no audience but ourselves.

My friends bring joy to so many.
This party is a way to recognize each other
And celebrate what we do for the world.

Standing in the middle of the room
Reveling in the human beauty of it all,
Hearing what the hours of practice and days of travel,
Songs written, shows good and bad,
The time in the studio
All come to

I get lost in the sound.
Reminded of what I love most about
Being a musician,
I thank the gods I never quit
And I pray that I'm always

A part of this circle.

Schoenhut, 2018

The Risk of the Plugged-In Life

If you are always pursuing what lights you up
The chances are that every now and then
You will stick your finger in a light socket.

When you know what you love
And you are truly connecting with it,
You feel alive, charged.
This approach to life is loaded with risk.
It can completely blow up in your face.

But I think it's worth the gamble
Because it just might work out.

Intensity, 2016

Fearing Your Gift

1.
We fear our gift
Because we know that to truly embrace
The best part of who we are
And really be that person
Means we might have to change our story
About what we do,
Where we spend our time,
What we love.

2.
When I'm young, I want to be a rock star,
Onstage, bright lights, famous.
I make a good run at it, and do pretty well.

Now, years later, I find myself just as lit up,
    if not more,
Sitting and writing a song with someone who
    doesn't even write songs.
Whether it's a soldier, a homeless teenager just
    off the streets of Newark,
A bunch of Israelis and Palestinians,
    a friend who just lost a partner.
I want to find their story, make it sing.

This is very different from what I thought my life
    would look like,
The one I spent years trying to build and maintain.
When I do this work, there's no spotlight,
    no stage or applause.
Just music, without the music business.

My career is not what I imagined it would be.
It's better.

3.
When I first start looking for and finding
Different ways to use songwriting,
I don't talk about it much.
Even though I know that
It makes a difference,
Has an impact, moves people,

There's a part of me that worries
What people in the music world will think of me,
    of this work.
They might say that I haven't "made it."
I must be sinking, grasping
Or God forbid, teaching.
I wonder if I will lose all my credibility,
And with it, their respect.

For a long time, I struggle to admit even to myself,
Much less others,
That I love this new work,
That I have a certain knack for it — a gift,
    you might say.
On the surface, it seems so far from my
    original plan
That I have little context for it.

It takes several years to relax into the fact
That this new work ignites me in an
    uncharted way,
Bringing together a lifetime of effort, craft,
Searching for a story, digging for the emotion,
That truth of a moment
And turning all that into a song that lives.
The difference is that before,
All the effort was directed inward, toward me,
    my story.
Now it's external, focused toward someone else.

4.
Once I commit to moving in this new direction
And truly own what I can (and can't) do,
When I peel back the skin from
My desires, my abilities,
Being honest about what I want,
I change
And my story is forever different.

5.
I'm made stronger when
I throw my arms around all the disparate pursuits
That catch my focus
Not separating, but gathering together and
    holding close
My scattered curiosities,
Making them one,
Constantly tacking toward the place where
I'm most creatively charged
And most openly challenged.

Out there, I've nothing to be afraid of.

Past all the self-inflicted arguments
And second thoughts,
What others think about my work
Is irrelevant.
I just do the work,
Write the songs,
Keep moving.

6.
Fearing your gift is really fear of allowing yourself
    to shine.
It's choosing static over change,
The known pattern, even if it's not right,
Instead of the possibility of a better you.

We create a roadmap for ourselves
When we're young.
And it gets us where we are today.
But how we arrive here is history.
That same map may not apply tomorrow.

If that past
Points you in a new direction,
And you don't follow it
Out of fear of failure
Or that you might look silly,
Well, that's the making of a hollow life.

Open up.
Step out into the wind.
You're here for a reason.

We're counting on you.

Starhead, 2015

Following spread:
Leaves, Paris, 2013

ACKNOWLEDGMENTS

I'd like to think that I put this book together on my own,
But there were more than a few people always
In the back of my mind while I was writing.
I constantly wondered what they would say;
If they'd agree I was on the right track.
They are:

Radney Foster. Mary Gauthier. Boo Hewerdine. James and Sharon House.
My dad, Granvel Smith. His father, Earl. My son, Eli.
Mentors Ron Fierstein and Kip Krones. Tim Mathews.
Musical guides Roscoe Beck, Stewart Lerman and Michael Ramos.
For the early song inspiration, Rodney Crowell and Jerry Jeff Walker.

My love, partner and best friend, Haley Rushing,
Who put up with long hours talking about this book,
And my long disappearances to work on it.
She put it into the shape you see now.

Larry and Erin Waks let me use their house in Marfa, Texas for weeks at a time
While I wrote, edited and worried.

Cyndi Foster and Kevin Connolly read a few early drafts,
And helped me see how these could be used in the world.
With a view that only a 19-year-old can bring,
My daughter, Willa, delivered a staggering ego punch and
Forced me to take a long look at the reason behind each piece.
I remain lovingly humbled and grateful.

For editing, Sabrina Barton saw it first.
Tamara Saviano set me straight on some mechanics
And connected me with Lynne Margolis,
Who edited the text and struggled to instruct me on the proper use
Of the comma, which I, for the most part, ignored.

Big gratitude to DJ Stout for his patience, push and long-term collaboration.

Thanks to Warren Zanes for the foreword;
Matt Lankes for the cover photo;
Sean McKenna for a great deal of encouragement.

Bill Worrell connected me to Irie Books.
Thanks to Gerry and Lorry there, for taking a chance.